MORTAI ANIM

GW01452669

On Religious Unity
by
Pope Pius XI
1928

St Athanasius Press

1

ISBN-13: 978-1533155276

ISBN-10: 1533155275

St Athanasius Press
2016

Specializing in Reprinting Catholic Classics!

MORTALIUM ANIMOS

ENCYCLICAL OF POPE PIUS XI
ON RELIGIOUS UNITY

TO OUR VENERABLE BRETHREN
THE PATRIARCHS, PRIMATES,
ARCHBISHOPS, BISHOPS, AND
OTHER LOCAL ORDINARIES
IN PEACE AND COMMUNION WITH
THE APOSTOLIC SEE.

Venerable Brethren, Health and Apostolic Benediction.

Never perhaps in the past have we seen, as we see in these our own times, the minds of men so occupied by the desire both of strengthening and of extending to the common welfare of human society that fraternal relationship which binds and unites us together, and which is a consequence of our common origin and nature. For since the nations do not yet fully enjoy the fruits of peace - indeed rather do old and new disagreements in various places break forth into sedition and civic strife - and since on the other hand many disputes which concern the tranquility and prosperity of nations cannot be settled without the active concurrence and help of those who rule the States and promote their interests, it is easily understood, and the more so because none now dispute the unity of the human race, why many desire that the various nations, inspired by this universal kinship, should daily be more closely united one to another.

2. A similar object is aimed at by some, in those matters which concern the New Law promulgated by Christ our Lord. For since they hold it for certain that men destitute of all religious sense are very rarely to be found, they seem to

have founded on that belief a hope that the nations, although they differ among themselves in certain religious matters, will without much difficulty come to agree as brethren in professing certain doctrines, which form as it were a common basis of the spiritual life. For which reason conventions, meetings and addresses are frequently arranged by these persons, at which a large number of listeners are present, and at which all without distinction are invited to join in the discussion, both infidels of every kind, and Christians, even those who have unhappily fallen away from Christ or who with obstinacy and pertinacity deny His divine nature and mission. Certainly such attempts can nowise be approved by Catholics, founded as they are on that false opinion which considers all religions to be more or less good and praiseworthy, since they all in different ways manifest and signify that sense which is inborn in us all, and by which we are led to God and to the obedient acknowledgment of His rule. Not only are those who hold this opinion in error and deceived, but also in distorting the idea of true religion they reject it, and little by little. turn aside to naturalism and atheism, as it is called; from which it clearly follows that one who supports those who hold these theories and attempt to realize them, is altogether abandoning the divinely revealed religion.

3. But some are more easily deceived by the outward appearance of good when there is question of fostering unity among all Christians.

4. Is it not right, it is often repeated, indeed, even consonant with duty that all who invoke the name of Christ should abstain from mutual reproaches and at long last be united in mutual charity?

Who would dare to say that he loved Christ, unless he worked with all his might to carry out the desires of Him, Who asked His Father that His disciples might be "one." And did not the same Christ will that His disciples should be marked out and distinguished from others by this characteristic, namely that they loved one another: "By this shall all men know that you are my disciples, if you have love one for another"? All Christians, they add, should be as "one": for then they would be much more powerful in driving out the pest of irreligion, which like a serpent daily creeps further and becomes more widely spread, and prepares to rob the Gospel of its strength. These things and others that class of men who are known as pan-Christians continually repeat and amplify; and these men, so far from being quite few and scattered, have increased to the dimensions of an entire class, and have grouped themselves into widely spread societies, most of which are directed by non-Catholics, although they are imbued with varying doctrines concerning the things of faith. This undertaking is so actively promoted as in many places to win for itself the adhesion of a number of citizens, and it even takes possession of the minds of very many Catholics and allures them with the hope of bringing about such a union as would be agreeable to the desires of Holy Mother Church, who has indeed nothing more at heart than to recall her erring sons and to lead them back to her bosom. But in reality beneath these enticing words and blandishments lies hid a most grave error, by which the foundations of the Catholic faith are completely destroyed.

5. Admonished, therefore, by the consciousness of Our Apostolic office that

We should not permit the flock of the Lord to be cheated by dangerous fallacies, We invoke, Venerable Brethren, your zeal in avoiding this evil; for We are confident that by the writings and words of each one of you the people will more easily get to know and understand those principles and arguments which We are about to set forth, and from which Catholics will learn how they are to think and act when there is question of those undertakings which have for their end the union in one body, whatsoever be the manner, of all who call themselves Christians.

6. We were created by God, the Creator of the universe, in order that we might know Him and serve Him; our Author therefore has a perfect right to our service. God might, indeed, have prescribed for man's government only the natural law, which, in His creation, He imprint-

ed on his soul, and have regulated the progress of that same law by His ordinary providence; but He preferred rather to impose precepts, which we were to obey, and in the course of time, namely from the beginnings of the human race until the coming and preaching of Jesus Christ, He Himself taught man the duties which a rational creature owes to its Creator: "God, who at sundry times and in divers manners, spoke in times past to the fathers by the prophets, last of all, in these days, hath spoken to us by his Son." From which it follows that there can be no true religion other than that which is founded on the revealed word of God: which revelation, begun from the beginning and continued under the Old Law, Christ Jesus Himself under the New Law perfected. Now, if God has spoken (and it is historically certain that He has truly spoken), all must see that it is man's duty to believe absolutely

God's revelation and to obey implicitly His commands; that we might rightly do both, for the glory of God and our own salvation, the Only-begotten Son of God founded His Church on earth. Further, We believe that those who call themselves Christians can do no other than believe that a Church, and that Church one, was established by Christ; but if it is further inquired of what nature according to the will of its Author it must be, then all do not agree. A good number of them, for example, deny that the Church of Christ must be visible and apparent, at least to such a degree that it appears as one body of faithful, agreeing in one and the same doctrine under one teaching authority and government; but, on the contrary, they understand a visible Church as nothing else than a Federation, composed of various communities of Christians, even though they adhere to different doctrines, which may even be incompatible one with another. Instead, Christ our Lord instituted His Church as a perfect society, external of its nature and perceptible to the senses, which should carry on in the future the work of the salvation of the human race, under the leadership of one head, with an authority teaching by word of mouth, and by the ministry of the sacraments, the founts of heavenly grace; for which reason He attested by comparison the similarity of the Church to a kingdom, to a house, to a sheepfold, and to a flock. This Church, after being so wonderfully instituted, could not, on the removal by death of its Founder and of the Apostles who were the pioneers in propagating it, be entirely extinguished and cease to be, for to it was given the commandment to lead all men, without distinction of time or place, to eternal salvation: "Going therefore, teach ye all nations." In the continual carrying out of this task, will any element of strength and efficiency be wanting to the Church, when Christ Himself is perpetually present to it, according to His solemn promise: "Behold I am with you all days, even to the consummation of the world?" It follows then that the Church of Christ not only exists to-day and always, but is also exactly the same as it was in the time of the Apostles, unless we were to say, which God forbid, either that Christ our Lord could not effect His purpose, or that He erred when He asserted that the gates of hell should never prevail against it.

7. And here it seems opportune to expound and to refute a certain false opinion, on which this whole question, as well as that complex movement by which non-Catholics seek to bring about the union of the Christian churches depends. For authors who favor this view are accustomed, times almost without

number, to bring forward these words of Christ: "That they all may be one.... And there shall be one fold and one shepherd," with this signification however: that Christ Jesus merely expressed a desire and prayer, which still lacks its fulfillment. For they are of the opinion that the unity of faith and government, which is a note of the one true Church of Christ, has hardly up to the present time existed, and does not to-day exist. They consider that this unity may indeed be desired and that it may even be one day attained through the instrumentality of wills directed to a common end, but that meanwhile it can only be regarded as mere ideal. They add that the Church in itself, or of its nature, is divided into sections; that is to say, that it is made up of several churches or distinct communities, which still remain separate, and although having certain articles of doctrine in common, nevertheless disagree concerning the remainder; that these all enjoy the same rights; and that the Church was one and unique from, at the most, the apostolic age until the first Ecumenical Councils. Controversies therefore, they say, and longstanding differences of opinion which keep asunder till the present day the members of the Christian family, must be entirely put aside, and from the remaining doctrines a common form of faith drawn up and proposed for belief, and in the profession of which all may not only know but feel that they are brothers. The manifold churches or communities, if united in some kind of universal federation, would then be in a position to oppose strongly and with success the progress of irreligion. This, Venerable Brethren, is what is commonly said. There are some, indeed, who recognize and affirm that Protestantism, as they call it, has rejected, with a great lack of consideration, certain articles of faith and some external ceremonies, which are, in fact, pleasing and useful, and which the Roman Church still retains. They soon, however, go on to say that that Church also has erred, and corrupted the original religion by adding and proposing for belief certain doctrines which are not only alien to the Gospel, but even repugnant to it. Among the chief of these they number that which concerns the primacy of jurisdiction, which was granted to Peter and to his successors in the See of Rome. Among them there indeed are some, though few, who grant to the Roman Pontiff a primacy of honor or even a certain jurisdiction or power, but this, however, they consider not to arise from the divine law but from the consent of the faithful. Others again, even go so far as to wish the Pontiff Himself to preside over their motley, so to say, assemblies. But, all the same, although many non-Catholics may be found who loudly preach fraternal communion in Christ Jesus, yet you will find none at all to whom it ever occurs to submit to and obey the Vicar of Jesus Christ either in His capacity as a teacher or as a governor. Meanwhile they affirm that they would willingly treat with the Church of Rome, but on equal terms, that is as equals with an equal: but even if they could so act. it does not seem open to doubt that any pact into which they might enter would not compel them to turn from those opinions which are still the reason why they err and stray from the one fold of Christ.

8. This being so, it is clear that the Apostolic See cannot on any terms take part in their assemblies, nor is it anyway lawful for Catholics either to support or to work for such enterprises; for if they do so they will be giving countenance to a false Christianity, quite alien to the one

Church of Christ. Shall We suffer, what would indeed be iniquitous, the truth, and a truth divinely revealed, to be made a subject for compromise? For here there is question of defending revealed truth. Jesus Christ sent His Apostles into the whole world in order that they might permeate all nations with the Gospel faith, and, lest they should err, He willed beforehand that they should be taught by the Holy Ghost: has then this doctrine of the Apostles completely vanished away, or sometimes been obscured, in the Church, whose ruler and defense is God Himself? If our Redeemer plainly said that His Gospel was to continue not only during the times of the Apostles, but also till future ages, is it possible that the object of faith should in the process of time become so obscure and uncertain, that it would be necessary to-day to tolerate opinions which are even incompatible one with another? If this were true, we should have to confess that the coming of the Holy Ghost on the Apostles, and the perpetual indwelling of the same Spirit in the Church, and the very preaching of Jesus Christ, have several centuries ago, lost all their efficacy and use, to affirm which would be blasphemy. But the Only-begotten Son of God, when He commanded His representatives to teach all nations, obliged all men to give credence to whatever was made known to them by "witnesses preordained by God," and also confirmed His command with this sanction: "He that believeth and is baptized shall be saved; but he that believeth not shall be condemned." These two commands of Christ, which must be fulfilled, the one, namely, to teach, and the other to believe, cannot even be understood, unless the Church proposes a complete and easily understood teaching, and is immune when it thus teaches from all danger of erring. In this matter, those also turn aside from the right path, who think that the deposit of truth such laborious trouble, and with such lengthy study and discussion, that a man's life would hardly suffice to find and take possession of it; as if the most merciful God had spoken through the prophets and His Only-begotten Son merely in order that a few, and those stricken in years, should learn what He had revealed through them, and not that He might inculcate a doctrine of faith and morals, by which man should be guided through the whole course of his moral life.

9. These pan-Christians who turn their minds to uniting the churches seem, indeed, to pursue the noblest of ideas in promoting charity among all Christians: nevertheless how does it happen that this charity tends to injure faith? Everyone knows that John himself, the Apostle of

love, who seems to reveal in his Gospel the secrets of the Sacred Heart of Jesus, and who never ceased to impress on the memories of his followers the new commandment "Love one another," altogether forbade any intercourse with those who professed a mutilated and corrupt version of Christ's teaching: "If any man come to you and bring not this doctrine, receive him not into the house nor say to him: God speed you." For which reason, since charity is based on a complete and sincere faith, the disciples of Christ must be united principally by the bond of one faith. Who then can conceive a Christian Federation, the members of which retain each his own opinions and private judgment, even in matters which concern the object of faith, even though they be repugnant to the opinions of the rest? And in what manner, We ask, can men who follow contrary opinions, belong to one and the same Federation of the faithful? For example, those who affirm, and those who deny that sacred Tradition is a true fount of divine Revelation; those who hold that an ecclesiastical hierarchy, made up of bishops, priests and ministers, has been divinely constituted, and those who assert that it has been brought in little by little in accordance with the conditions of the time; those who adore Christ really present in the Most Holy Eucharist through that marvelous conversion of the bread and wine, which is called transubstantiation, and those who affirm that Christ is present only by faith or by the signification and virtue of the Sacrament; those who in the Eucharist recognize the nature both of a sacrament and of a sacrifice, and those who say that it is nothing more than the memorial or commemoration of the Lord's Supper; those who believe it to be good and useful to invoke by prayer the Saints reigning with Christ, especially Mary the Mother of God, and to venerate their images, and those who urge that such a veneration is not to be made use of, for it is contrary to the honor due to Jesus Christ, "the one mediator of God and men." How so great a variety of opinions can make the way clear to effect the unity of the Church We know not; that unity can only arise from one teaching authority, one law of belief and one faith of Christians. But We do know that from this it is an easy step to the neglect of religion or indifferentism and to modernism, as they call it. Those, who are unhappily infected with these errors, hold that dogmatic truth is not absolute but relative, that is, it agrees with the varying necessities of time and place and with the varying tendencies of the mind, since it is not contained in immutable revelation, but is capable of being accommodated to human life. Besides this, in connection with things which must be believed, it is nowise licit to use that distinction which some have seen fit to introduce between those articles of faith which are fundamental and those which are not fundamental, as they say, as if the former are to be accepted by all, while the latter may be left to the free assent of the faithful: for the supernatural virtue of faith has a formal cause, namely the authority of God revealing, and this is patient of no such distinction. For this reason it is that all who are truly Christ's believe, for example, the Conception of the Mother of God without stain of original sin with the same faith as they believe the mystery of the August Trinity, and the Incarnation of our Lord just as they do the infallible teaching authority of the Roman Pontiff, according to the sense in which it was defined by the Ecumenical Council of the Vatican. Are these truths not equally certain, or not equally to be believed, because the

Church has solemnly sanctioned and defined them, some in one age and some in another, even in those times immediately before our own? Has not God revealed them all? For the teaching authority of the Church, which in the divine wisdom was constituted on earth in order that revealed doctrines might remain intact for ever, and that they might be brought with ease and security to the knowledge of men, and which is daily exercised through the Roman Pontiff and the Bishops who are in communion with him, has also the office of defining, when it sees fit, any truth with solemn rites and decrees, whenever this is necessary either to oppose the errors or the attacks of heretics, or more clearly and in greater detail to stamp the minds of the faithful with the articles of sacred doctrine which have been explained. But in the use of this extraordinary teaching authority no newly invented matter is brought in, nor is anything new added to the number of those truths which are at least implicitly contained in the deposit of Revelation, divinely handed down to the Church: only those which are made clear which perhaps may still seem obscure to some, or that which some have previously called into question is declared to be of faith.

10. So, Venerable Brethren, it is clear why this Apostolic See has never allowed its subjects to take part in the assemblies of non-Catholics: for the union of Christians can only be promoted by promoting the return to the one true Church of Christ of those who are separated from it, for in the past they have unhappily left it. To the one true Church of Christ, we say, which is visible to all, and which is to remain, according to the will of its Author, exactly the same as He instituted it. During the lapse of

centuries, the mystical Spouse of Christ has never been contaminated, nor can she ever in the future be contaminated, as Cyprian bears witness: "The Bride of Christ cannot be made false to her Spouse: she is incorrupt and modest. She knows but one dwelling, she guards the sanctity of the nuptial chamber chastely and modestly." The same holy Martyr with good reason marveled exceedingly that anyone could believe that "this unity in the Church which arises from a divine foundation, and which is knit together by heavenly sacraments, could be rent and torn asunder by the force of contrary wills." For since the mystical body of Christ, in the same manner as His physical body, is one, compacted and fitly joined together, it were foolish and out of place to say that the mystical body is made up of members which are disunited and scattered abroad: whosoever therefore is not united with the body is no member of it, neither is he in communion with Christ its head.

11. Furthermore, in this one Church of Christ no man can be or remain who does not accept, recognize and obey the authority and supremacy of Peter and his legitimate successors. Did not the ancestors of those who are now entangled in the errors of Photius and the reformers, obey the Bishop of Rome, the chief shepherd of souls? Alas their children left the home of their fathers, but it did not fall to the ground and perish forever, for it was supported by God. Let them therefore return to their common Father, who, forgetting the insults previously heaped on the Apostolic See, will receive them in the most loving fashion. For if, as they continually state, they long to be united with Us and ours, why do they not hasten to enter the Church, "the Mother and mistress of all Christ's

faithful"? Let them hear Lactantius crying out: "The Catholic Church is alone in keeping the true worship. This is the fount of truth, this the house of Faith, this the temple of God: if any man enter not here, or if any man go forth from it, he is a stranger to the hope of life and salvation. Let none delude himself with obstinate wrangling. For life and salvation are here concerned, which will be lost and entirely destroyed, unless their interests are carefully and assiduously kept in mind."

12. Let, therefore, the separated children draw nigh to the Apostolic See, set up in the City which Peter and Paul, the Princes of the Apostles, consecrated by their blood; to that See, We repeat, which is "the root and womb whence the Church of God springs," not with the intention and the hope that "the Church of the living God, the pillar and ground

of the truth" will cast aside the integrity of the faith and tolerate their errors, but, on the contrary, that they themselves submit to its teaching and government. Would that it were Our happy lot to do that which so many of Our predecessors could not, to embrace with fatherly affection those children, whose unhappy separation from Us We now bewail. Would that God our Savior, "Who will have all men to be saved and to come to the knowledge of the truth," would hear us when We humbly beg that He would deign to recall all who stray to the unity of the Church! In this most important undertaking We ask and wish that others should ask the prayers of Blessed Mary the Virgin, Mother of divine grace, victorious over all heresies and Help of Christians, that She may implore for Us the speedy coming of the much hoped-for day, when all men shall hear the voice of Her divine Son, and shall be "careful to keep the unity of the Spirit in the bond of peace."

13. You, Venerable Brethren, understand how much this question is in Our mind, and We desire that Our children should also know, not only those who belong to the Catholic community, but also those who are separated from Us: if these latter humbly beg light from heaven, there is no doubt but that they will recognize the one true Church of Jesus Christ and will, at last, enter it, being united with us in perfect charity. While awaiting this event, and as a pledge of Our paternal good will, We impart most lovingly to you, Venerable Brethren, and to your clergy and people, the apostolic benediction.

Given at Rome, at Saint Peter's, on the 6th day of January, on the Feast of the Epiphany of Jesus Christ, our Lord, in the year 1928, and the sixth year of Our Pontificate.

PIUS XI

Printed in Great Britain
by Amazon